From the Heart

STEVEN ROSE

AuthorHouse™ LLC
1663 Liberty Drive
Bloomington, IN 47403
www.authorhouse.com
Phone: 1-800-839-8640

Published by AuthorHouse 06/02/2014

ISBN: 978-1-4969-1455-2 (sc)
        978-1-4969-1456-9 (e)

authorHOUSE®

The Screeching Fiddle

When the Dues are Due
It might not be paid in the coin of the Realm
Or in the bullets whistling by your head
Nor in the scars of wounds, all hidden and healed
Or in the lashes taken as a child
Not the tumble taken down the stairs, just to break a leg.
It was not paid by the sleepless nights in the cauldron of the Blues
Or when near-drowning off the stern of a ship going down fast in a vortex whirl of fire and flames.
I have been searching far and wide to find the reason
I'm alive and can only conclude.
I have paid the full bill,
When the dues are due.
Some of these troubles
I have I've brought upon myself.
Most of them, I believe, is because of circumstance.
Now that I have made, sincerely, all of my Amends.
I patiently await for all of those who have stabbed me in the back to come to me and say,
"Sorry about that". I presume they'll take it to the grave, without regret.
All I know to be true is I have paid in full when the dues are due.
No, it was not paid by the coin of the Realm
Nor by the Hurricane that blew my home away,
or by the countless betrayals made by people
I have helped.
No broken hearted haunting that the thirst for whiskey couldn't slake.
No pills, no heroine, cut to thin could take those memories away.
Even though I'm done with that, the ash and smoke remain.
I'm ready now for moments of joy and happiness again.
Because when the dues were due, I paid them all in full.
The slate is clean now,
I'm almost feeling brave.
Cause I have been forgiven and have been learning to do the same.
All the dues will be fully paid, when I go to my grave.

At The Carnival Fair

I'll take you to the carnival fair.

We'll ride twice every screaming ride there.

I'll win you a giant Panda Bear.

We'll smother our face in cotton candy,

As we're dazzled by the blinking lights.

On the promenade, with the Barkers Pointing out all the sights.

We'll take snapshots, and make funny faces in the picture booth.

We'll go through the Haunted House and skip a beat or two of our hearts.

Reshape our bodies in the funny mirror.

You'll look like Stan, me like Ollie,

Watching the laughing children ride the ponies.

We'll carry a handful of helium balloons to have a balloon fight

And watch them, latter, climb into the starry sky.

We'll be laughing and smiling as we hold hands and kiss,

As the booming fireworks light up the valley,

Amidst the din of the mystified crowds.

Later, we'll conjure up the dimming memory.

Oh what a night we had, At the Carnival Fair.

Message in a Bottle

Shall we ever see each other?

Could it ever be that a sincere man

hear the oratory of Pericles shouted

from the Acropolis hill,

on the portico of the Parthenon,

Thoughts thrown across the immeasurable of time

Could it ever find a home within the heart of a stranger

Perhaps, I'm destined to never know,

which is to say, I'm merely a shadow.

and the sea that is wrangling is inside of me

I have a empty bottle of a Portuguese Rosa

Quite good it was and therein placed these ramblings

hit the cork with all my might

and tossed it forcefully into the brewing sea.

A Far Away Voice

I want you to think of me as a far away voice

that comes into your hearing range saying

"You are Beautiful"

For over 20 years or so

I have been in love with you

Your breathing,

your movement,

your thoughts,

your hardiness

And your ethereal softness of your skin

So I have spent my dreams making love to you.

You would shout as I would shout in orgasmic delight.

I have lusted after you, as any man would do.

I live a secret life that could only honor my best friend's wife

I live the loyalty of humble servitude and amidst the morning clouds

I shall always be, forever, a little distant voice.

Don't You Think It's Time

The day has a sky of cloudless blue

The night is lit by a half Moon

assigning shadows to the stones of tombs

Don't you think it's time to leave your little room?

The air is light with the lilting sun the air

is sultry with tobacco and tears In this room

is humanity and safe from fears and I understand

why you'd rather not leave Because it is here

you can contemplate and breath upon

all of God's given things I see the fear in your eyes

some kind of childhood trauma some kind of killing going on

some kind of hanging from that lonesome tree

Yet here you are, now, all these years later and unsure

Don't you think it's time to leave your little room ?

And journey forth to a new adventure?

The Gold Diggers Dream

He will take you to every parade

he will take you to every Ice Escapade

He'll fly you out to

Vegas and let you lose a mil

You can motor on his yacht to San Moritz,

Lear it up to sunny Vale for a skiing trip,

Go to all the charity balls, where he'll be wearing a full dress Tux

and you will be wearing a designer gown

that will highlight your sparkling jewels

You'll Waltzed Through the night,

drinking champagne and dine

on choice meat that tastes like bliss

and you'll end the night melting

your insincere body to him and your phony kiss.

Well that's the life of a

Gold Diggers Dream and your proud of it.

Your favorite mansion is the one with the pool.

You'll be lounging there leafing through

all the beauty magazines that describe every nit, tuck and new boobs too!

So by the time you reach your seventies,

you'll be the picture of youth.

There'll be a time, you can't wait, when the old man dies,

or he may take off with a pretty young thing

Either way you look at it, you'll end up rich and slighted and pompous too.

You'll buy the largest monument,

in the one percent cemetery where all the rich are kept

You know the one, where the howling winds erupt from hell.

I used to take my hammer and hit it true on the nail

I used to take a car engine and make it purr, not flail

I worked, as well as build you a house,

it was built to the tee from your design.

I worked, and sweated all day and night till I broke my back

and ended upon with dirty clothes, to do the task

I loved you dearly and kept all my marriage vows

I didn't hear the preacher say for better

or I'm getting the hell out of here.

So when you're on your death bed, if you still have a mind,

You can ponder on the pride, that you've gone so far

on a lie from the holler of the mountains, where you wore hemp clothes.

And where you grew up on dandelions and coon and squirrels.

and no matter who you crushed on the way,

you found what you were looking for

You found the song of The Gold Diggers Dream.

The Girl With The Little Red Rose Tattoo

I quaffed way more than my share

in a wrist to wrist,

chest to breast

pub called Bertha Bartholomew's

when my eyes gazed upon a little red rose tattoo

on a perfect barmaid's fulsome breast

She was a mirage of the Moulin Rouge

her green eyes, her smile and gregarious laugh,

wiped the tears from my eyes and healed my broken heart.

She, reverently served me the best single malt whiskey,

and downed a few herself all through the night.

She asked me to stay behind when Bertha's shut down,

There was something she needed to say in quiet and privacy,

and besides as young as I was,

never seeing a tattoo on a girl before,

like a scientist,

I wanted to study the red so deep

and see if there were any thorns hidden in the deep green

of the convoluted stem around the leaves.

Then she held me tight and I kissed her little red rose tattoo

with spinning passion and made love beyond the sun

gliding through the tapestries windows.

We were friends for many years,

till time stole her away.

But I'll never forget-her seaside tavern voice

and how our tears mingled in joy and sorrow and passion.

Every time I dream and see that little rose tattoo,

I remember, how in my youth,

that long ago at Bertha Bartholomew's,

Heaven visited me here,

on Earth.

I Believe

I believe in Jezus and his parables

I believe in magic and the sea

I believe that, one day, the blind will see

I believe that grief and sorrow will surely be relieved

I believe in triumphal love

I believe in infinity

I believe that EMC2 and God are one

But mostly I believe in you

A Ship Upon A Painted Ocean

I lay here lost in the voices in my head

seeking for some psychic revelation to help me arise from this bed

The window world of shadowed trees and singing birds

cannot divert the pendulum to commit to life

or cessation from the world nor mitigate my cowardness

I once was a conduit of mystical powers and saved many lives

and witnessed the souls rise out of bodies of the ashamed dead to dimensions way beyond mortality

I was the ultimate friend and intriguing lover, kind, faithful and steadfast through any storm

Yet rebellious to control in any way or form

Yet here I lay so helplessly, paralyzed, and blind

which maters not a whit to history or endless time

So what matter, if there is no hope the doctors say to dwell on other thoughts and things will turn alright.

And I tell them hope diminishes not.

though wracked with exhausting pain.

I leave it to my imagining to fight for life allied with a power greater than my own

To hope beyond fate's full notion that I shall always be

A painted ship upon a painted ocean.

And so it came to be.

Thank You ,
Stan L.Ollie

Just The Keeper of The Story

Just inside the screaming ambulance

I was thrown into the hospital.

My heart was playing parradittles like Jean Krupa with the upbeat by Buddy Guy.

To celebrate their treating me so well,

they stopped my heart.

As they hovered over me with their lightening paddles,

I pronounced what a good night's sleep was never had,

and had a thought.

Maybe, in a delayed way, one could die from a broken heart.

Even though it was a long time ago,

in the year that Lennon died.

I bought you a car as a surprise.

You left the next day and my world fell apart,

I felt a twisting knife in my chest.

I couldn't breathe especially taking that little girl away

who came crying and left happy and contented .

For three years I was Daddy.

You left me for, some unknown to me, psychopathic jailbird, fresh from prison.

Later I heard he knocked you up and knocked you around and threatened to kill that little girl.

By then I was drowning in cheap vodka, or I'd been on Death Row.

Am I merely in some delayed zone and dying of a broken heart?

One for you and Greta, one for Dawn and JoAnne,

One for Tom, Steve, Glenn, Mary, Larry, Ina, all gone.

Heart be still now.

The river of tears have left me nearly numb.

I'm just the keeper of story now.

Of how sweet love can break your heart and somehow you survive.

When The Day Is Done

Oh when the day is done

When the baby is sighing in her sleep.

Now I get a chance to say

You made this day so beautiful.

How your laughter has healed near forgotten wounds.

The Odd dreams where I used to drown in a Safire sea

are refracting into diamonds and cutting into past notions

of the memory I had, of life and love.

It leaves a mark, like a solo violin in a symphony.

When the silence comes.

I hear a simple phrase,

I'll love you till the end of time

Knowing that time is like a bird,

flying away from me.

When I meld with you it's all tingles and goose bumps and exploding stars,

then sleep and the sunrise.

Oh yesterday is done.

The baby cries to announce the new beginning day.

Only longing for your sea blue eyes and silky skin

and breast to feed her the milk of the sun and earth and moon.

You smile at me,

it will be a busy day to come.

While working under the blazing sun I'll be dreaming

When the day is done.

Beautiful Dream

These were all the words I said as a child.

I am happy to report,

I drove them all crazy.

Why, even my sweet grandmother,

a Gauche girl and a friend of Rachel Carson,

and the sweetest person I ever met,

threatened me with the guillotine if I asked her "why" one more time.

She taught me Mozart chords on Thanksgiving and Christmas

On the Bekenstein that grew old in the corner of her parlor.

I received an invitation to my favorite niece's engagement party.

She's in her early 40's,

has several grown or nearly grown children.

I have always loved her for her adventurism,

her unique artistry and her tenaciously savvy disposition.

My note ended with a fragment of a Kalil Gibran poem-------

Love is a magic ray

emitting from the burning core of the soul

and illuminating the surrounding earth

It enables us to perceive life

as a beautiful dream

Between one awakening and another

Buckets of Rain

Can't seem to set it aside these buckets of rain,

Rainfall torrents spinning like wheels down the highway.

Buckets of seasons passing by

In a four masted ship stern high in a skyscraper wave.

heading into the sunrise heaven towards

God's saving grace

Can't set it aside, these buckets of tears

that river of Blues spreading in a spectrum of colors

spraying through a tea time lace,

that paints the laugh lines on your face.

Can't set it a side

The ivory keys of your Bechenstein

whose scales possess my heart

When I am on my knees,

begging for forgiveness.

in a bucket of rain where I found a morning pearl,

where an eagle flew from the treetop.

I especially could not set aside my love for you

and all that has been,

and shall be.

Comrades in Vietnam

I threw my body up one my comrades in Vietnam as a medic trying to stop the bleeding.

Most of them died and my boy is riddled with bullets and shrapnel yet a few survived.

18 that I know of as of this day and I ate a lot

peyote and acid and waved the healing flag high.

I was a murderer at the age of my youth.

I pray for forgiveness and have dwelt upon the amends that I still must make.

Yet today I feel no anger nor pity or self loathing.

All I feel is suicidal, do to frustration and pain.

I went blind again,

except for the opaque shadows that come to me from time to time.

All systems are deteriorating without rhyme or reason,

yet right on time.

And worst of all, I feel no purpose for living.

What does this have to do with you?

Because I know a thing or two,

and you know as well how to conquer suffering with joy,

You have done wonders and I want some of what you got to see me through.

I Can't Take That Touch Away

I can't take that touch away, nor could I

It remains to unfettered fate,

from the alpha to the omega,

in the enigma we shall never know.

But there are hints, like a bird in the sky,

and the vision in a dream upon awakening

as well as the prayer that is fulfilled

Yet why do I feel so hopeless that the cause of the future

will be to heal, when the past is one of invisibility today

I shall not be able to take my touch away.

My heart is like a book of mystery,

who's last chapter always unread.

The prism's rainbow, circles the galaxy tells me,

I cannot take your touch away.

Adapt, change, live, die, love, hate.

Cry into the river

that flows into the salted ocean, inexplicable

Yet in my heart and body I cannot take my touch away.

So it shall be, till the last breath,

when I shall metamorphose

Into a bright light unseen dimension of energy.

It is said that love maybe troubling,

amidst stunning moments of joy

Why, my dear, you must ride it like a roller coaster,

and get closer to the stars,

Knowing, ultimately that life is but a riddle,

we spend our life to solve.

but as we study the sky and yearn for endless love

It's true to say

I can't take that touch away.

Love

by Steve Rose

I love your kisses

I love your smile when you look into my eyes

I love your cold hands and feet,

when I warm them all between my thighs.

I love your laughter and your gracefulness in the storm of life

I love your ears and your neck below

It makes me believe that I could never stop kissing you

A thousand times.

I've told you I only love you

That you are the one, the only one that God has told me to love.

I love your sighs when we make love.

Could you imagine the happiness of having a child?

The joy the hope, the dreams unfathomable?

I love your kisses.

The Moon is On the River

The moon is on the river,

I saw it there before I fell asleep

somewhere a midst my unfinished prayers.

It appeared like a diamond

mystery and sounded like a scream,

a triple high 'c' trumpet announcing

'I am free'.

Yes I'm free

Cause the moon is on the river,

laughing a time.

Somewhere down the alley

the symphony is tuning up.

The violins are chasing the French horns

while the percussion are tying up the trombones

and oboes dive into the holy rose.

It might be the coming Mozart or Beethoven

or a mantra from Tibet

Oh My it's from the sky and the sinew

of the heart. Yes it's true and will not change ,

at least for tonight,

That the Moon is on the river.

As bright as love could ever be.

The Repair Shop

Broken wing

How can I survive

When I cannot fly?

Broken heart

How can I survive

When I cannot love?

Memories abound, yet,

I cannot live on glories past.

Oh glory, glory it was,

Like the sunrise kiss of the ocean's waves

Seemingly creating a pathway to infinity.

Where there are no troubles, only euphoria.

The place wherein all is bright and restored

Where we molt our egos rein

And metamorphose into pure energy

All I know is death's gleam

Stands in the way.

In the meantime

I fervently search in every way

For the building

Whose marquee displays

The Repair Shop

There Comes a Time

There comes a time,

where there are no words to express the feelings you have,

You'll be looking into someone's eyes, amidst the full moon and a million stars.

The truck is loaded and gassed up,

for the miles and miles that you'll be going,

Into Life's great change, not knowing,

if be into a hurricane or a sunrise as red as Mars.

Who can truly describe the journey of a million miles,

nor the unique complexity of

A piercing light, that colors everything in sight in the tragic comedy of life?

All I know is that I will never be coming back,

for the rest of it, I have no words.

Yet I can hand you a manuscript of words

The Ode to Love and Sacrifice,

But like winds blowing through the trees,

there are no rimes for War and Peace,

Nor a description of a shadow of the thoughts or pleas,

of a man found on his knees,

On the beach under a stormy cloud,

whose thunderclaps and rain and hail mingles with his sobbing tears.

Every day is a book of dreams.

where words of magnificent love,

or sorrows blight,

Cease to exist in full form.

There are no words to truly enlighten,

The travels of time and life as it forwardly moves in the day,

To destiny Into the Divine Creator's

Stunning bright light.

Words on Awakening

I'll remember you

when there's sunrises like these

where shadows play on the sugar sand beach,

and all the birds take flight to dive

for breakfast, that's just out of reach

when the first beams of light

knock you off your feet

and I won't ever again

meet you on the street

yes, I'll remember you

I'll remember you from the morning songbird

to the hoot of the owl

when I awake with a tear in my eye

and don't know why

but it must be true

that I'll be missing you

and in all the time that travels by

Yes, I'll remember you.

An Understanding

Against the memory of all my dreams I apply
I was placed in the prevue of truth
Against my fantasy of the past exuberance
I know that I am not the key to your happiness

The suitcases taken on the journey are stacked so high
and nothing exists unentangled with time
Yet time is the key
To a profound understanding between you and I
Here in lays a mere glimmer of a martin sunrise
like your painting of the savannah trees

The wind and love will blow where it blows
Happiness is rooted in the fabric of each ones soul
all else is a gamble, like crossing a rapid river wide

I know you and
I have a growing understanding and I
I must trust in my fantasy and dreams guided
by the creator
That tells me

What better love could be a friendship?
And
what better friendship could be an understanding love?

Ancient Window Blinds

The sunlight squeezes through the ancient window blinds.

The mist of dawn giving over to the colors of the stratosphere

I am lying here with the knowledge of 12,000 days and a trillion snapshots

wondering what magic the day will bring

I hear the symphony of song birds among the whisper of the distant surf

Please I beg of you please on this morning,

I yearn for sleep to reunite with a dream I was having before being so rudely interrupted.

All I know is that I do not know

Return me back to that lullaby

I will just throw a blanket over my head, making sure my nose sticks out

and forget for awhile that the sunlight ,now ,is squeezing

through the ancient window blinds.

Angels

There can never be too many Angels;

The sun has broken into the horizon.

Another day is born.

The dawn and singing birds promise a day different than before.

The world is spinning

on its blue axis trying to kiss the sun,

while half the world is starving and at war.

There can never be too many Angels.

Let them sit at my table

Let them help me spread my wings.

Let me watch the children run.

Let this darkness be gone

Let them lead me to the light.

With all the lying, crying and dying

there can never be too many Angels.

Bring the morning on.

Let me step into the sunlight.

Let the apparitions, darkness, and regrets

for what could have been done, all be gone.

There is no end in sight.

only their love and guiding light.

There can never be too many Angels.

As I See It Greta

The sun has traveled to the other side of the earth.

In the dim light I sit on your little bed.

I see you sleeping.

As your tiny chest rises up and down,

I hear you, child of three, curling up.

sighing as you travel down your road of dreams.

I'm glad you know nothing of the warrior's way.

or the psychopathic greed and cruelty,

but only know the Angels that swirl around your head in a yellow halo.

What a snapshot of time it proved to be.

that night I sang to you that lullaby of life.

In which I sang to you that, simple me, would love you forever.

That, my dear Greta has and shall always remain true.

even as I wonder whatever happened to you?

As I see it Greta, in that moment in time,

like a snapshot in my mind that shall never be forgotten.

The lessons we learned together stands out in my repertoire.

of how I love a beautiful woman and her magnificent child.

37

Bloody Mary Sunday

Bloody Mary Sunday

Or is it Monday?

I was dancing, laughing and crying the days and nights through arriving here,

hunched over a giant, strong, dogs breath,

Bloody Mary, patching up a lost soul hang over,

wondering who the hell has hit me with this hammer and who has broken in half the hill

outside my window?

I don't remember much,

except for that last kiss when I swore my undying love for you and bid You Adieu while

stumbling down the steps, far away from you.

Here to wrestle with a piercing arrow that entered my heart swimming in tarnished lust

And now clinging to my gluteus maximums I pledge no allegiance to a wounded heart,

nor to a new hole in my arse.

Yet I still swear to you my undying love.

The bottle, now empty and with the last giant, strong, breath Bloody Mary at my lips.

I pray anew.

Don't You Think It's Time

The day has a sky of cloudless blue

The night is lit by a half Moon

assigning shadows to the stones of tombs

Don't you think it's time to leave your little room?

The air is light with the lilting sun the air

is sultry with tobacco and tears In this room

is humanity and safe from fears and I understand

why you'd rather not leave Because it is here

you can contemplate and breath upon

all of God's given things I see the fear in your eyes

some kind of childhood trauma

some kind of killing going on

some kind of hanging from that lonesome tree

Yet here you are, now, all these years later and unsure

Don't you think it's time to leave your little room?

And journey forth to a new adventure?

Forlorn

When I look into your crystal eyes

I see the earth wind fill the bold sails of souls

which moves me closer to the edge.

I tremble in fear before the sirens of the stormy sea.

I close my eyes and clutch my sword to slay the death of innocence.

Blindness has overtaken me like a gallant fool,

as I fall down on my bed of stone

Do I have a chance to love you with all heart and lust,

down the grotto where Christ's blood mixes with the prayers and

dust I will light a candle there on the battlefield,

in the blazing shadows of Joan of Arc.

I died many times yet remain reborn to forlorn love.

A warrior once and now a vapor.

Hard and Soft

I am a mixture of the hard and soft.

Can't stand to be compared to the past or a shadow of the lost?

I am a blend of love and hate.

Primordially composed of a lions courage,

yet full of fear to let it be.

I am the creator of confusion and the orderly way.

The Earth revolves around the sun.

One minute I'm on solid ground and in the next am drowning in quicksand.

Love is going to be the way it will be.

You are wild and I was drinking myself to death with such hope.

Maybe it's time to say

That that's the way it goes.

know you love me, neither of us unkind.

The shadows are too real

I haven't much to offer.

I'm too tired to love and fight anymore.

All I know is that you are much like me

A mixture of the hard and soft.

The Vase

A foot below the volcanic ash lays a broken vase

The Insomniacs Dream

The foghorns blow as mournful as distance.

The God of the Holocaust grimaces,

overlooking the silhouettes of the city that craves at the harbor

I find myself on a bridge under a copper sunset diminishing into shadows

The fiery stars appear covered by dark clouds

till they seem to be black holes in the back of my mind.

Light just like, has been withheld from me.

Lone sailors huddle in sea side stone

taverns bending with gin

Tin cup dreams of stormy seas and fears of death.

As well as dreams of a kiss when day is done,

for love and fornication's sake

for candlelight and incense and for faithful love

I wait, on a swinging bridge without scripture,

without terror

All I hear are the fog horns blaring, the songs of the city.

Meet Me When The Rescue Is Over

The Phone is clanging in the foreground,

as I sleep on a dive sofa

The dawn is ghostly gray upon the window

I am holding on tenaciously to a entertaining Technicolor dream.

while the phone is clanging me back to cold reality.

I pick up the tele and hear your sonorous voice say,

I am listening to the tick tock of the grandfather

clock I tried to be brave. It's dark and,

I'm holding a shiny razor blade and my wrist are bare.

Don't you move I'll be right there.

Don't make a move I'm on my way

I know it's hell to love a millionaire who you love so much, yet he doesn't care

Do you remember when I knocked the pistol from your head.

Must love and passion parade in the last day in a cavalcade of insanity?

It was good of you to call me

I who have no answers but only know how to rescue the one I love.

OLD LANG ZINE

OLD LANG ZINE with you,

though lately I shrink inside my hermits habit

and shed a few sentimental tears for what has past nor be forgotten.

Yet I rejoice that the New Year has struck.

catapulting me over the calamities,

which here to for,

has inhabited so many of the past seasons.

The Owl

SShadowy, dark hue in a half moon night,

in the center of countless stars.

Crickets rubbing, unknown,

unseen rustling from woods to fence,

while overhead a deep tumbrel,

piercing hooting of an owl.

He is announcing his dominance of the night ,

to me the stranger and to my cat.

Stubborn tenacity among the lacy shadows, hallucinatory,

as a childhood picture of Jesus,

Like a windup clock,

whose insatiable ticking in the silence,

reminds me of The Pit and the Pendulum

In a Janis Joplin half moon night is the piercing

scream of a unseen owl announcing,

survival, survival not the racket of despair;

but the powerful drumbeat of a heart filled with gratitude and hope.

How Did YOU Become So Beautiful?

How did you become so beautiful? I think I know the answer.

Because there are the stars and sky and the rise and fall, the tears and laughter,

the sea the sun the towers and the sculptures.

The paintings in all colors to delight, the birds in flight over all the animals of the Ark.

The fishes in the ocean deep among all that dwells in infinity

How did you become so beautiful? I think I know the answer.

It's because The Creators hand has touched you with Love

I'm so grateful he has shared with me that magnificent love,

with me that love for all the exquisitely beautiful things.

Like the silver throated voices of bells that hold the earth in a spell.

Like the rainbow illuminating the midday sky

like the rare embrace of the sun and moon in the sunrise horizon

to let you know God's love is close, sometimes as close as in the center of the heart.

As I look at you, as your beauty fills my heart and soul

I know and want to sing the song of truth

I know why you have become so beautiful

The Spring And You

The stormy sky has been driven to the ocean

The blizzard, the boney chill, the ice encrusted trees of the valley

has given up its hopeless grip.

Now daffodils and iris and blue bells

with the operatic birds sing of kinder days to come.

It's time to be free, time to breath in a certain rhythm.

The sun gets closer. Yesterday has died.

Tomorrow is full of magnificent hope

The earth erupts into life and love, and it's so wonderful to be alive on

this God given day.

The stones in the road have gone, whence they came.

Endless stars have replaced the stormy sky and though you are gone,

beyond amends there will never be a time when I won't love you.

I'm caught up in memories subtle web where I held you next to my heart

like a silky breeze of spring.

I have been unable to let you go in all the seasons full,

Especially in spring whence you taught me how to love

The stormy sky has driven

the winter to the ocean .In my dreams I will see you among

the treasures; love and hope will bring me through this beautiful world

as I see the spring and You.

There'll be a time

There'll be a time when the storm will subside.

There'll be a day when sight will come back to the blind.

There'll be a time when broken hearts will be mending.

When love will arrive around the hidden bend?

It won't be today or tomorrow, but I know it will be someday soon.

Sure as the sun will be rising.

Sure as the full moon lights up a mysterious path.

You'll be led to a land of love and forgiveness.

By the hand you'll be guided to a place of peace, where your heart will mend.

Today is St Patrick's Day

Today is St Patrick's Day,

The winter on the earth shall be gone soon.

Soon a bit of green will invade

and we'll just have to break into

a beautiful song

like the darling wee birds

at the top of the trees.

We'll break into a beautiful song.

Today is St. Patrick's Day.

We'll roar like a lion

and like bears stop our hiding.

We'll resume our conversations

with the earth and the moon and the stars.

We'll be dancing and spinning

and shouting to the heaven's.

That it's time, yes it's time,

for a new love.

Words on Awakening

I'll remember you

when there's sunrises like these

where shadows play on the sugar sand beach,

and all the birds take flight to dive

for breakfast, that's just out of reach

when the first beams of light

knock you off your feet

and I won't ever again

meet you on the street

yes, I'll remember you

I'll remember you from the morning songbird

to the hoot of the owl

when I awake with a tear in my eye

and don't know why

but it must be true

that I'll be missing you

and in all the time that travels by

Yes, I'll remember you.

What A Grand Day For A Picnic

I knew long before the dawn, in a sleepless night,

that today would be a grand day for a picnic.

We could go to Joe's for subs and our drinks,

then sit at the river at a picnic benches there

and watch the boats and every kind of seabird,

and let river breezes blow through our hair.

We would have quite a conversation there,

from the colors in the rainbow to the soap opera stories

of the cosmos and the complicated entangling affairs out there.

You know the changes that have been in your own life are immense.

I hope it turns out to be the most delicious,

sweet and juicy mango like a paradise anew.

And thank God for the Valium that helps to get you through.

In My Secret Heart

There are a million words of poetry written in the 16th century,

no one do rhyme, and there's countless feeling,

past the spectrum of the Galaxy, that lives, beyond the grip of time.

They all live, in splendid mystery.

In My Secret Heart.

Forgive me for my lying ways, and my cheating like a fool.

My eyes that are nearly blinded, and here I give you my greatest gift of all.

The loving sacred box of broken tools.

For you who do not know me, yet you who knew me best.

I keep the Golden Key, which unlocks, everlasting,

Love to the world, The Love that resides, within, My Secret Heart.

In MY Secret Heart----inspired by Leonard Cohen

Sailing

Once I went a sailing on the sea according

To the Captains charts, we'd end up at the Plymouth Bay

Where all our fevered dreams lay in wait to peal like a 'full throated bells",

upon the shores of freedom's surf.

If this well wormed ship and if luck would chance it, and sink at first

Nor'easters were not spliced into a thousand shards of torn off nails and wood.

Faith and hope and love be our master then

and like the 8 mile wind in our sails, configure our destination.

My Love to June Lynd and Barbara Olsen, my protective and guiding Angels.

Thank you to my mom Elizabeth S. Rose.

Poetry inspires and cleanses my soul. With each word I hope to bring inspiration to others.

Printed in the United States
By Bookmasters